LUXURY

LUXURY

POEMS

Philip Schultz

W. W. NORTON & COMPANY

Independent Publishers Since 1923

NEW YORK | LONDON

For information about permission to reproduce selections from this book, write to Permissions, W. W. Norton & Company, Inc., 500 Fifth Avenue, New York, NY 10110

For information about special discounts for bulk purchases, please contact W. W. Norton Special Sales at specialsales@wwnorton.com or 800-233-4830

Manufacturing by Berryville Graphics
Book design by JAM Design
Production manager: Lauren Abbate

Library of Congress Cataloging-in-Publication Data
Names: Schultz, Philip, author.
Title: Luxury : poems / Philip Schultz.
Description: First Edition. | New York : W. W. Norton & Company, [2018]
Identifiers: LCCN 2017033688 | ISBN 9780393634686 (hardcover)
Classification: LCC PS3569.C5533 A6 2018 | DDC 811/.54—dc23
LC record available at https://lccn.loc.gov/2017033688

W. W. Norton & Company, Inc.
500 Fifth Avenue, New York, N.Y. 10110
www.wwnorton.com

W. W. Norton & Company Ltd.
15 Carlisle Street, London W1D 3BS

1 2 3 4 5 6 7 8 9 0

I put this book here for you, who once lived
So that you should visit us no more.

— CZESLAW MILOSZ

FOR ROBERT

CONTENTS

LUXURY

PARAPHERNALIA

I'm in my study, worrying about essentials,
like car keys and wallet with all its accouterments
to prove my behavior is legal and matches my age.
As I get older more seems to be needed.
My dog, Penelope, has her own, leash, collar
and tags plus toys and treats to meet the occasion.
Even my car is one, I imagine, with all its gadgets
to measure how much of itself is used up.
Family, of course, of which I'm one, and carry
everywhere in photos, arguments and worries,
especially when alone. And yes, the past with
all its trappings, résumés, expectations and
resentments, cluttering the view of the present,
which I seem to have less to do with lately,
standing as I do off somewhere nearby,
confused as to what just occurred, and why.
Yes, I'm quickly aging, feeling all filled up
with box scores and the ubiquitous world
of politics and tragedy. Right now, for instance,
my sixteen-year-old son is doing homework,
listening to *SportsCenter*, while my wife is on
the phone advising our older son on college classes,
half-listening to NPR relay the latest refugee calamity.
And here I am, worrying about a future my sons
will help make, while my soul waits patiently
at the door, hoping I'll remember my sunglasses,
car keys and Penelope, in my hurry to be obsolete.

AARDVARKS

It's summer and the Jitney is packed,
every seat taken, except for the one
five rows up, in which a burly man
has barricaded his window seat
with a briefcase and jacket, an act meant
to confront others with his superiority.
Munching chips and guffawing at
a YouTube video of an obese woman
riding a scooter down a country road,
towing a younger obese woman
in a wheelchair, he reminds me
of a neighbor's dog that would steal
and bury our dog's bones, then growl
defiantly on his side of our fence.
He's the reason I'm sitting back here
next to the toilet, thinking about Pythagoras,
who believed our souls ended up inside
the bodies of animals selected as rewards
and punishments. Well, the three giggling girls
stretching their legs into the aisle every time
the shy attendant passes, making him stutter
apologies in a Slavic accent – orangutans, probably.
Sequestered back here between work and family,
thought and dreaming, I'm slowly evolving into,
say, an aardvark, the last living representative
of a nocturnal, burrowing species hurling down
the highway inside a bus whose shell is camouflaged
as a vodka ad, on its way to a barricaded future
on the far side of a fence where all our significance is buried.

IGA

It's one week after Sandy
and Mrs. Cobb, our mailman's aunt,
who lived in the Halloween house on Sherrill Road
that burned down, is ahead of me in line,
hands in her hair, screaming.
Betsy, the cashier, is telling the assistant manager,
Peggy, that all she did was say her peaches
aren't the ones on sale. Mr. Brim, the sourpuss
who owns the pizzeria on North Main, yells
from behind me, "Just give her the damn peaches!
A dead deer's on my garage, my backyard's a lake,
we're still at my sister-in-law's and I'm not hollerin' my head off!"
I offer to pay and Betsy snorts, "You!?"
because two years ago I refused to make a third donation
to her Baptist choir and her god isn't the forgiving kind.
Now Rudy, the manager, is here, angry
not to be among his friends the chips and donuts in aisle 6.
"Good!" Mr. Brim groans, "now everyone's here!"
Actually, almost everyone *is* here, JJ,
the deli air drummer who hums R&B and slices
everything thin, Fergus the cart gatherer
whose tattoos depict angry biblical patriarchs
and Benny in produce who lost 84 pounds eating sardines
and Cocoa Puffs and has iPhone photos to prove it,
all come to see if this is another catastrophe
that will keep us up all night, watching our kids sleep
in the living room, praying for the wind to stop,
the roof to hold, that last insurance bill got paid,
fearing our ignorance and pettiness is to blame,

that if we were just a little more humble in the hearing
and sublime in the doing, as Saint Augustine suggested,
we could all go back to sleep only one donation
and the right peach shy of deliverance.

AT THE MANHATTAN SOCIAL
SECURITY OFFICE

The mind seeks what is dead, for what is living escapes it.
— MIGUEL DE UNAMUNO

I'm practicing the stoic art of insouciance,
not because I prefer not thinking about
what signing up for Medicare means,
or why so many who came after me are being
called first, but because downstairs
my soul was examined for signs of violence
and duplicity. Its fatigue and ambivalence
weren't visible, apparently. In the next row
a man is telling a girl bobbing to an iPhone
to sit still before the guard returns.
When I was her age signing up meant going
to Vietnam, which meant practicing
the Zen art of vanishing. At the windows
a blind man is asking why he didn't receive
his disability payments in prison,
he needs his "sustenance." Behind me,
another man is asking to see my paper,
he's looking for work, he says. Happy
to be free of "Afghanistan: What Could Work,"
I hand him my *New York Review of Books.*
Bismarck said explaining was a weakness.
As her father explains the necessity
of securing her future, the girl squirms.
She fears only boredom. I feared everything.
In five months my father would die
and mother and I would live on the $200 a month
his Social Security paid. At the windows

the blind man is practicing the existential art
of groveling, exposing the stitches on his scalp
to a clerk who's practicing the cynical art
of indifference. The girl's soul, hovering near
the ceiling, is enjoying its moment of radiance.
My soul, fretfully pacing the watercooler,
is practicing the fatalistic art of understanding
that nothing can be done about Afghanistan,
that in order to influence the future we must kill it.

THE WESTERNS

Once again,
Randolph Scott is thinking out loud on TV
about the end of freedom,
God, mercy, why
barbed wire fences no longer hold back
old or new grudges, rabid squatters,
the wagonloads
of grueling pilgrim faith
in an ever-westward-expanding destiny,
while once again
I'm up late remembering
the lacquered sunsets
on the Paramount's patched screen
Saturday mornings, me
and ten to fifteen other hoodlum sons
of immigrant dreamers aloft
in the filthy froth of the balcony,
surrounded by the ear-popping
fall-to-your-knees-
and-say-hallelujah serendipity
of the swooning music.
Westerns
were what we wanted, couldn't get enough of,
all those standoffs between
postwar rectitude vs. existential greed
feeding our burgeoning hunger
to be part of
the great American rhapsody.
Everyone mumbling,
believing only in gullibility,

Technicolor,
eradicating evil,
owning everything – is this why
every ten minutes the plot questioned
everyone's manhood for no reason whatsoever,
the town drunk drank,
the hero sought revenge from a flashback
(that'd murdered his entire family in slow motion),
why everyone believed in
the rewards of futility,
the solace of violence,
the dignity of misfortune,
waited endlessly for the always late,
just around the bend,
steeped in appetite,
in irresistible grief,
beaten to a pulp
utterly insulted point to arrive,
hoping
it'd tie everything together, finally, maybe,
why
all these peculiar curlicues
are whirling through my sleepy brain,
because nothing
and everything has changed,
and my tiny moment is also quickly passing
while the end is taking me somewhere
the beginning never wanted me to be?

AGE APPROPRIATE

Sometimes,
mystified by the behavior
of one of my sons,
my wife will point out
if it's age appropriate,
making me wonder why
I still shout at ballplayers on TV
and argue with the dead.
Last week, my oldest son,
with a wild pitch, turned
my left ankle into an eggplant.
I didn't yell at the doctors
who refused my insurance,
or get angry with a friend
who told me to soak it
in bourbon and garlic. No,
I read Montaigne who said
self-revelation is the purpose
of discourse, which, in his day,
meant knowing whether
to be flattered if a friend
didn't use a food taster,
or amused if a witch cast a spell
of weeping on an in-law.
Blaise Monluc, the king's
lieutenant general during
the civil wars, Montaigne says,
threw so many hanged Protestants
down a well you could reach in
and touch the top one's head. Yes,

Monluc, who was fond of saying:
"When the scaffolds are full, use trees,"
knew what was appropriate.
On occasion I'll run into a lobby
to avoid greeting a friend,
not because my mind vanishes
and I can't remember his name,
which is true, but because I
must flee what is darkest in me.
In other words, when evicted from
a strange lobby into a stranger street,
where every scaffold is full
and bodies dangle in the long
blue sorrow of the afternoon,
without context, explanation, or sympathy,
it's good to know, even momentarily,
how to live, among the relevant,
the passionate, and the confused.

GREED

My ocean town struggles
to pick up leaves,
offer summer school,
and keep our library open.
Every day now
more men stand at the railroad station,
waiting to be chosen for work.
Because it's thought
the Hispanics will work for less
they get picked first,
while the whites and blacks
avoid each other's eyes.
Our handyman, Santos,
who expects only
what his hands earn,
is proud of his half acre in Guatemala,
where he plans to retire.
His desire to proceed with dignity
is admirable, but he knows
that now no one retires,
everyone works harder.
My father imagined a life
more satisfying than the one
he managed to lead.
He didn't see himself as uneducated,
thwarted, or bitter,
but soon-to-be rich.
Being rich was his right, he believed.
Happiness, I used to think,
was a necessary illusion.

Now I think it's just
precious moments of relief,
like dreams of Guatemala.
Sometimes, at night,
in winter, surrounded by
the significant silence
of empty mansions,
which once were cottages,
where people lived their lives,
and are now owned by banks
and the absent rich,
I like to stand at my window,
looking for a TV's futile flickering,
always surprised to see
instead,
the quaint, porous face
of my reflection,
immersed in darkness,
its one abundance.

HOW I BECAME A TEACHER

She sat there quietly,
across the kitchen table,
playing solitaire, each
sighing breath rising and falling,
the green shine of her eyes
turning opaque, each descent
of her shoulders lowering me,
her left shoe tapping a tune
I never recognized. Not once
did I interrupt, ask for something
the way father always did.
I sat across the snowy world,
slowly mastering the art of
disappearing into someone else.

THE KISS

For Jack Ceglic and Manuel Fernandez-Casteleiro

In a sense,
Jack and Manuel were starting over again.
Jack, a Romanian Jew who designed our house,
drank our kids' "concoctions"
made out of everything on a restaurant's table,
which we wouldn't do,
and Manuel, who shared his amazement
at a perplexing world
while surviving Cuba, communism and AIDS,
got married at City Hall not long after two men could.
To help them celebrate,
Monica and I brought a fancy bottle of champagne
we could never find a reason to open before.
As is the custom, we kissed after my toast,
while they just looked at each other, curiously.
"Never in public before," Jack said.
Okay,
I know what it feels like to see myself
through the harsh light of another's eyes.
To be the *other.*
Suddenly,
we were they and they us, if you know what I mean.
I mean: objectified.
Relax, there's no point to be made.
Even notarized, love is never normal or wise,
and no one knows how to behave,
or hasn't felt despised.
It doesn't matter that my toast was celebratory,

that I'm saying now what I couldn't say then.
What matters is they kissed, finally,
quite elegantly,
and we all enjoyed the splendid dinner Jack made.

CAKES

My wife makes porcelain sculptures of cakes,
each the size of an actual cake,
delicious monuments to every occasion,
if edible only by the imagination.
On each an object: a bird, feathers, stones,
teeth or piles of tiny primeval people,
struggling, it seems, either to be more defined
or less conspicuous.
One, a slice with a single tiny figure
balancing itself awkwardly on top,
mystified by its absolute aloneness,
wondering what happened to all the others.

Sometimes
I watch her standing there, arms akimbo,
staring at her theater of absurd desserts
crowding the table in the living room,
thinking perhaps of the uncelebrated child
hidden inside the wife and mother,
inside the artist, each surprised,
if not delighted at what was made
out of nothing but faith
that what lies hidden
in each birthday and anniversary
can be grasped, cherished,
and eaten.

THE WOMEN'S MARCH

So many mothers are here, daughters and granddaughters.
Mine's been dead for nineteen years but somehow
managed to come. I'm seeing her everywhere,
in the pleased-with-itself smile of the little girl
riding her father's shoulders, holding a sign
announcing girl power and the beginning of the
Women's Century, in the don't-mess-with-me look
of the much-pierced young woman in black
who appears to have finally found her cadence,
in the excited green-gray eyes of the old woman
in a wheelchair being pushed along at quite a clip
by, I assume, her grandson, who looks absolutely
mesmerized. And just ahead is the forceful stride
of the black drummer banging away for all she is
and wants to be, using everything she has to make
a point about strength and willfulness and sacrifice
that maybe only women have the right to make,
having made all of us, shared themselves so completely.
A point about going too far and not far enough,
about time, and the pain it brings, and yes, here I am,
older than I ever intended to be, enjoying the ringing
in my ears, remembering being lifted into the air
by my mother, trembling with joy, as she enfolded
me into the hospitable wings of her peasant apron.
Yes, she's here, marching with all the others, all of whom
understand what's being asked of them, one more time.

SADNESS

Suddenly
for no reason I can point to
everything feels afterwards,
stoic and inevitable,
my eyes ringed with the grease of rumor and complicity,
my hands eager to hold any agreeable infatuation
that might otherwise slip away.
Suddenly
it's evening and the lights up and
down the street appear hopeful,
even magnanimous,
swollen as they are with ancient grievances
and souring schemes. The sky,
however,
appears unwelcoming,
and aloof, eager to surrender its indifference to my suffering.
Speaking of suffering,
the houses – our sober, recalcitrant houses – are swollen
with dreams that have grown opaque with age,
hoarding as they do truths
untranslatable into auspicious beliefs.
Meanwhile,
my loneliness,
upon which so many personal laws are based,
continues to consume everything.
Suddenly,
regardless of what the gods say,
the present remains uninhabitable,
the past unforgiving of the harm it's seen,

while
the future remains translucent
and unambiguous
in its desire to elude me.

THE DIFFERENCE BETWEEN

Something vibrant and shiny
is always hurrying away from me,
some kind of possibility
of fidelity to what, and whom,
I meant to be. Something
vaguely necessary, even essential.
The difference between
being late and early,
open and closed, bereft
and on the verge
of something more interesting.
An opulent refrain, say,
trying to maintain,
and keep up with what's vanishing
around the corner from
where I stand, waiting
to be a little less solemn
and arcane,
a little more concrete. Someone
possessed of a quality
one can acknowledge,
even forgive. In any case,
there I am, remain,
a thought leaning
just out of reach,
glistening like a fish
at the back of my psyche,
infused
with vibrant possibility.
Is this why I remain

faithful to everything
I've lost along the way?
I never wanted to be me,
I don't think. Once
a beguiling idea
disguised as a question
to which no answer
exists.

A MOMENT

A measurement of time
in which desire
and regret live side by side.
A request for further deliberation.
A pause designed
to forestall malignancy;
to regain one's reasonableness
and equilibrium. A schism
in which conviction and mediocrity
conspire
to eliminate each other.
A channel through which guilt flows
unashamed. An allotment
for those who've used up
all their other choices.
An expectation
of contentment or annihilation.
A reality
without windows or doors,
without time.
A wall
behind which nothing more
waits to happen.
A hedge against excess or charity.
A desperate cry.
A grain of sand.
A last breath.
A vast opportunity.
A plea to begin over again.

WHAT TO BE AFRAID OF

Fate, Mom believed, hated us even more than God.
Which is why we must never cry, she said.
Not after the Hildebrand twins hung me upside down
from Mrs. Polowska's cherry tree, pushed me off
her garage roof through Mr. Zwas's porch window,
who chased us with a pitchfork, a Red Sea squirting
from my thumb, would I. Not when Lefty McBride
kicked me in the stomach three times, and I yanked
Danny Enright off his bike by his hair, and got my eyeballs
thumb-scrubbed by Ollie Baskin's older brother Hymie,
my nose autographed by a sidewalk. Not when cops
picked me up, explaining the way things worked:
"Know what to be afraid of, son," and I skipped school,
snuck into the RKO's balcony to be a forlorn cowboy
and lunatic gangster, who also belonged nowhere,
not where they came from or anyplace they were,
cared only about getting even and catching a break,
suffered fits of self-loathing rage. Yes, they also knew
what crying meant: letting it all in, surrendering to hope
and shame, a slave's longing for salutation and welcome.
It would all find you anyway, Mom said, even up here,
under painted stars, surrounded by swooning music,
strangled by history and poisoned by pride, with only
an illiterate God for company, who also knew that
once started it would never end.

SACRIFICE

A vest designed to explode.
An argument about God
and nothingness and shame.
An idea infused with hunger,
with hate spread over the pavement,
smeared along the wall, obscuring
every view and reflection. A theory
about liberation from the self;
about resignation and fulfillment,
surrender and glory. A photo
of a woman smiling at the men
she's about to obliterate; of a boy
walking brusquely toward his fate,
already eclipsed by time. A logic
stretched, pummeled and caressed
by death. A plea for God as sanctuary,
testimony and reward; for remaining
ordinary and alive and not shorn apart.
An argument, finally, between souls
and their bodies about being or not
gifts of God.

AT THE 9/11 MEMORIAL

There are so few trees.
Shade is necessary,
and merciful.
The fierce staring
and incurious silence.
The long winding lines
and frantic rubbings, posing,
the respectful attention
and clear blue eye of the sky –

this is a dour, elegant place,
where the essential and the excruciating
are at an impossible impasse,

where everything has already been said
and nothing seems to have always existed.

ENTHRALLMENT

the tenor sax cannibal
that makes you clean –

In memory of Michael S. Harper

You, a magic trick, still looming over me,
the fragile equilibrium and painful miscellany
of my every strategy for the sublime. I, jobless,
a draft-dodging manqué too terrified of your stature
in my eyes to look up. "Jews only think they're white,"
you said, trying to pull out of me all the embryonic pain
I sanctified, the strength I'd need to survive. Each of us
an apocalyptic neighborhood, a slave pierced with
a Hebrew longing for an ancient bloodstream,
Monk's "Always old, always new, always déjà vu."
Once, at a gathering to honor you, I tried but couldn't
find the words to thank you for your gift of encouragement.
You, the king of nightmare and responsibility, honorable
amendments to the history of tunes sung from the abyss;
me, someone also reaching "from pain to music great enough
to bring me back." Forty years and that cold antediluvian wind
from a P-town phone booth still despises me as you explained
why R ate snail poison, strangled himself in cellophane:
"He couldn't stop believing in the god of self-loathing."
All that night your words walked along frozen water,
grief an enslavement, an enthrallment. In the photo on
my desk we're young again, your eyes still singing songs
of love and hate and grace, your smile bursting with pride,
unafraid and willing to perform miracles. "Everything that is,
insofar as it is, is good," you quoted Saint Augustine. Yes,
for a moment we were, and one, meaning: all are saved or none.

GOOGLING OURSELVES

> You think yourself wise, proud Zarathustra.
> Then guess the riddle . . . Speak then: Who am I?
> — NIETZSCHE

These strangers with my name,
busy being kidnapped, embezzled,
honored, and dying at a frightening rate.
The cross-dressing exterminator convicted of rape
in Kensington, Ohio, sentenced
to seventy-two years without bail, the policeman killed
stopping a burglary in Thermopolis, WY – could they
have imagined a Florida painter with their name
communicating with extraterrestrials through sculptures
made out of railroad tracks, or being written about
in a poem by another member of their redundant family
for a reason none of us can explain?

Sometimes I fear I'm imaginary, don't really exist.
Catch myself wondering why I only seem to like myself
when, say, I'm wearing a teacher's face –
because I see myself only through others' eyes?
In that case, who am I really? Alone at night,
watching a ball game, I'm always surprised when
I speak to myself in the third person, wondering why
this man cares so much about something he plays no part in.

It's easier to wonder why Nietzsche sought
his soul's sympathy, a truth he knew he'd despise,
probably feared he wouldn't survive. To imagine him up late,
seeking his ever-evolving, unidentifiable self,
a past more inhabitable and less unforgiving,

anxious to know why someone with his name would say,
"Poets lie too much, who among us has not adulterated his wine?"

Late at night the Web is a dangerous swamp
of voyeuristic self-scrutiny and addictive impersonation,
the ego testifying for and against itself, seeking evidence
of triumph and complicity, sanction without malice,
pretext or God. Who is this man obsessively looking up
all his persona narrators, feeling like a hodgepodge,
trapped somewhere between heaven and earth,
spitting against the wind? Is it because he knows
he's getting closer to the end, will soon vanish
and become nothing? Is this why he's studying
everyone who answers to his name, because
one may have invented time or sympathy or God
and will love him, even momentarily, for who he is?

WELCOME TO THE SPRINGS

The dispersion and reconstitution of the self.
That's the whole story.
— CHARLES BAUDELAIRE

In memory of Robert Long

Here I am at your grave, again.
Often enough, driving around East Hampton,
taking short cuts you taught me,
this is where I end up. Okay.
But it's been ten years and I'm still not sure
what the Baudelaire quote on your stone means —
the soul's endless search for resolution,
our need to constantly redefine our illusions?
You know and won't say. What you don't know
is that we divided your things. I got
the Tiepolo poster and Elizabeth Bishop's
Geography III (noting her preference
for undercutting the tragic with a parenthesis).
By the way, there's a bright red Mercedes
in your driveway, you, who always just got by.
And your favorite sign, *Welcome to the Springs,*
is now at the center of a local controversy.
Some want to drop the "the" and just say *Springs* —
imagine that. Monica's new sculpture
has grown darker, as you said it would.
Eli is happy at Amherst, and Augie likes to write
(what a surprise!), while I've forgiven you, finally,
for not living to see the book you helped me write
get published. Only now do I understand that
it's not the resentment I regret, it's the shame.

Us, the oddest of sympathies – poetry friends,
vying for attention, encouragement, you, sober
six years, a historian of the art scene out here
on the East End of Long Island, I, married with
small kids, each writing again after a long silence.
"Write about this place," you'd say, "find its soul,
make it yours!" Yes, the ever-evolving, ever-munificent
light all your painters came here for – de Kooning
biking drunk down Springs Fireplace Road,
calling "Goodnight, Robert, best of luck."
Hey – last night on TV Bogart, playing
a drunken mercenary hiding out as a priest,
was told to seek sympathy among his own kind.
Well, all your personas: ex-drunks, art critics,
musicians, cooks and poets came to your funeral,
good food and music, but not much to say.
What role did I play that last night, watching you,
high on morphine, drop cigarettes into your lap,
swooning inside a cancer- and Coltrane-stained oblivion?
"What can I do?" you asked. "There nothing I can do."
Well, what didn't you do – chauffeuring James Brown
from Harlem to Montauk, high on Librium
you got from a Chelsea speed freak, cooking
your manic bouillabaisse stuffed with half
the Atlantic Ocean, spoon-dancing Getz
and Bud Powell, swollen with vodka and
dreams of Venice, your dinner riffs to Li Po,
Machado and Blake. How I liked your stories
of you, a gay teenager, wandering among your
MoMA pals, Goya, Rauschenberg and Francis Bacon,
learning to hide inside art's ecstatic parenthesis.
In any case, it's March, warm and wet and windy,
and this is where I live, here, where everything

lives in the eye and ear, and a silky frenzy
steeps the wetlands in testimony, in praise,
where the mating calls of osprey ricochet
between the loquacious silence of the dunes
and the cleansing sweep of moonlight,
where the souls of the dispersed dead pass,
making and remaking their silhouettes
one luminous, lost imagination at a time.

LUXURY

There is but one truly serious philosophical problem,
and that is suicide. All the rest . . . comes afterwards.

—ALBERT CAMUS

One

Be my stillborn son my son
—RALPH DICKEY

1

Sometimes
a hidden memory or thought
flings my right arm forward,
and I'll recoil,
as if struck by an invisible blow,
and cry out.
It's over in a moment,
but the cry,
elemental, fearful and contrite,
lingers
like a scent of decay.
That's when
all that has yet to happen
is erased
by what already has.

2

Here
in East Hampton, NY,
in the early winter ocean light,
where stuttering waves play variations
to the buoyant drift of the moon
and solitary fishermen cast wistful inquiries
into an upside-down shadowy kingdom,
reluctant,
while the sun is still offering its prospectus
for the new day,

to abandon their rituals of satisfaction
and return to the misgivings
of mailmen and roofers.

Here,
where clouds coalesce into vibrant silhouettes
and birds – gulls, ducks, piping plovers and the tentative Least
   Terns –
crisscross the sheer white sky,
my Border collie mix,
Penelope and I,
reverent
and adrift,
are also reluctant
to abandon this iridescent world
and return
to the disquiet of our familiar lives.

3
Perched
on the curb like a big roly-poly golden bird
a new 1955 Pontiac station wagon,
and Dad, triumphant,
waving at Mom, Grandma and me
to come out and see
its double hooded headlights,
big swerved tailfins,
shiny Ottawa War Chief hood ornament.
As we,
rotating clockwise,
are astonished by the automatic transmission,
cloth that shines brighter than leather,
eight powerful cylinders,

whitewalls reflecting a splendor
usually seen
in suburban driveways,
not deep inside Rochester, NY
in the inner inner city,
where snow buries spring
and memories of war still sour the air,
where everybody hates the sound of their last name,
and insolent curbs belittle
the reasonable trees.

Winking,
Dad slid me conspicuously
behind the wheel,
hollering, "How's that for luxury, kiddo!"

4
Saturdays nights
I went to hear R spin infinite spools
of biblical jazz prophecy
out of a miserable bar piano in our college town,
the kind that makes the floor weep
and the ceiling grieve.
R believed his pain was supreme,
that he was king, being
the son of a white mom
and the black man she cheated on
her white husband with . . .
Given his slave papers
and set adrift at eight in foster homes,
because, she explained,
he was too much of one thing
and not enough of another.

Thus, he became an orphan stillborn,
obsessed with white women,
the kind who came to hear him
use his genius to hate himself
and hate them,
up there, deep inside
each sullen puff of his cigarette,
his inner voice up-tempo dot-time scale riff
coming from
so far down
the only question left
was how much longer pain would sustain him,
he could live on nothing.

5
I was going to college in six months
when Dad had a stroke
and his doctor said: "If he doesn't stop working
he'll be dead soon. Since
he won't listen to me or your mother,
it's up to you now."

To an eighteen-year-old
death is an idea too arcane
to classify or confine.

Therefore,
no matter what I said,
he got up earlier each morning,
worked harder,
longer each day,
fell asleep at traffic lights,
over his meat loaf,

lost in a calculation
only he could resolve.

"We don't get along," I told Dad's doctor,
"he won't look at me."
"Yes," he said,
"but he's killing himself,
only you can save him now."

6

This Christmas,
a seventieth birthday present,
my wife and two sons took me
to Finca La Vigia,
Hemingway's house in San Francisco de Paula, Cuba.
where, I, among tourists from Canada,
China and Sweden, was utterly happy,
peering through fragile windows
at roped-off furniture, belligerent trophy heads,
decaying books and photos
of matadors and movie actors,
a ghostly Royal portable typewriter,
all
the vexed memorabilia
of death's foremost connoisseur.

Yes,
Hemingway,
whose stories I read while Dad was dying,
about fathers and sons,
codes of honor and courage
and gracious appetites,
the kind of stories I wanted to write,

with luminous sentences
unafraid to embrace the simplicity
of grief and disgrace.

Hemingway,
who like my father and R,
chose death,
would show me how to live.

7
Aloof,
bored perhaps,
slouched on a raised stage
on the first day of grad school,
R,
an example of what occurs,
the writing program director said,
when the peculiar
fuses with the hermetic
in the manic dreams of a genocide victim.
Yes,
R, haloed in praise,
having harvested
the stuttering strangled breath of the dead
in his translation of Paul Celan's "Deathfuge,"
singing: "Black milk of daybreak we drink it at evening . . .
            we shovel a grave in the air where you won't lie too
                cramped . . ."

Each word a dark psalm,
a thorn of mercy,
the naked center of nothing
that dwells in the almond.

Yes,
Celan, who three years later,
drowned himself in the Seine,
poet of the "human curl,"
the extinguished, splendid chasm,
carrying death under his arm
like a gift,
threshold
to threshold.

Is this why
one bright Iowa afternoon,
three cafeteria tables away,
R,
noticing me reading him,
said: "Yes, Celan,
Babel and Mandelstam
because Jews know death."

8
The ice cream parlor
Osiris, our guide, dreams of
will serve only one flavor,
his favorite, strawberry,
which tastes of the future,
sweet and quickly passing.
In Bulgaria they add buttermilk, he explains,
in St. Petersburg, vodka, to give a kick,
in Venezuela, coffee bean extract,
to improve the elasticity of the bladder
and unearth sour memories,
in Paris, licorice
for greater lasciviousness.

"Forgive me," he laughs,
"everyone here dreams of only one thing."

In Havana,
at night along the Malecon seawall
the young and old dance and fish,
make music with their eyes, hands and hips,
all and each owning
a piece of one delicious thing,
a feast of what's left of the imagination
after
all the souls of the masters,
the colonists,
the besieged and the seized,
leave,
leaving
only the keepers
of the revolutionary flame
whose visions are pure,
if vain and bloodthirsty,

while
all around us
herds of hungry stray dogs and chickens roam
obsolete highways
under fading, outraged billboards:
Socialism is Strong!
and *The US Embargo is genocide.*

and
voluptuous peacocks,
the ancient Buicks, Studebakers, Plymouths and Edsels
pass,

spraying black plumes
across
the blockaded sunset.

9
The light
at Louse Point
this cloudless February morning
is crystalline,
a harvest
of frozen silence,
the bleaching velvet rinse the painters came for,
hauling
their bereaved wonderment
and rituals of resignation and refinement,
their delusions and satisfactions.

Yes,
this is where I live,
in an ancient symmetry,
in the rhapsodic seep and spray of sea grasses,
here,
where the thrust and pulse of wind
instructs geese and swans on the physics of flight,
where land and sea begin
and the sky ends
and clouds perform dream symphonies
to the raucous applause of the waves,

here,
where the world begins again each morning
Penelope,
who usurps and dishonors nothing,

rolls around in the snowy sand,
kicking and howling with pleasure,
because,
according to the laws of her hierarchical nature
the scent of a dead gull
elevates
and excludes no one.

Two

He was too simple to wonder when he had attained humility.
—ERNEST HEMINGWAY

1

Sometimes
a noise I can sense
but not hear
ricochets
in a place in me
I can't name.
That's when
the darkness accentuates
all my feelings of guilt and shame
and I'm unable to distinguish
between misery
and nothingness.
When
all dignity vanishes
and nothing is left to say
or do,
be curious about,
or desire.
When
my mother's voice
pleads
for me to remember
everything
I live for.

2

Those of us
who live here year-round,
send our children to the local schools,
struggle during the summer influx
to sustain any semblance
of equilibrium.
Many attempt to get away,
rent their houses
and live in trailers,
while we all adapt
to being honked at,
scorned and beaten to a parking space,
hearing sirens scream
down one-lane roads
toward another fatal accident.

Mornings,
my wife runs along the ocean,
relishing
the light's slow sensuous descent
over fishing boats
that scrawl their signatures
along the burning horizon,
each an unexpected luxury,
not an entitlement.
The course, Aristotle said,
not to what is better
but to what
is better "started from."

3

On the first drive,
everyone inside the Pontiac
sat statue straight,
and wasn't rude or unkind.
Dad's lips didn't move,
his knuckles and thoughts didn't crack,
the past didn't once speak,
radio noise filtered out hurtful thoughts
and unclean memories,
Mom wore lipstick,
didn't resent
the lofty houses
and women we passed,
nobody complained, argued, pined for anything,
never once behaved
as if
they were an argument they couldn't win.

4

Once
in 1972,
after not having spoken in months,
R called to say
a big black bird perched on his shoulder
every time he tried to write,
questioning his every instinct
and desire to make something out of nothing,
even his right to console himself.
Neither poetry nor music would save him,
it said, he was only
forestalling the inevitable,

placating a grief
that would eventually defeat him.

I didn't know what to say
so I quoted Unamuno: "Self-compassion
widens into love of all that lives
and therefore wants to survive."
Each embryo was a phenomenon,
Unamuno said,
of singular longing,
a turning away
from the dark coil of agony.
Please, I pleaded,
remember the first time
his black foster mother placed
his fingers on a keyboard,
the astonishment
he felt in each note,
the joy of feeling original
and alive.
Music was his birthright, not pain.
Please, I pleaded,
assent to rhapsody,
the angels of revelation,
shun
this black bird of nothingness.

Yes, he said,
he understood,
but he didn't call to be saved,
he called to say goodbye.

5
Dad,
a descendant of Sisyphus on his father's side,
had a stone to push up a hill
each morning,
to watch as it rolled back down
each night.
Like Sisyphus,
he believed himself immortal
perhaps,
his mission to succeed
rendered him impervious to death.
Thus
he pushed the stone beyond
his capacity,
unaware,
that instead of defying death,
he was courting it.
Yes,
his punishment was also
the futility of endless labor,
but Sisyphus,
at the top of the hill,
looking down at fields of unending torment,
saw an opportunity for salvation,
and grace.
But Dad wasn't able to imagine
the absurdity
of endless toil
being rewarded
with relief
and wisdom

on the way down.
Thus,
his business failing,
his mind and spirit weakening,
on the way down,
instead of grace,
he suffered
only the pain
of endlessly imagining the way up.

At the age of seventy,
here I am,
teetering
on the edge of a hill,
perpetually having to reimagine
a legacy of disgrace
and the wincing it ignites,
a logic no less absurd
or cruel
than
the luxury of living perpetually
on the edge
of grace
and death.

6
Twenty-seven
is old enough
to know the difference between
suffering
and bewilderment,
boredom and pain,

but I didn't,
which is why
I visited Hemingway's grave in Ketchum, Idaho,
hoping to understand
the particular nature
of my desolation.
But it told me nothing
so I called his house
and his widow, mystifyingly,
invited me to lunch
and then took me to see his study,
where, nodding at his desk,
which overlooked high skies, valleys and mountains,
said, "That's where he did it,
with a shotgun, staring at all that . . ."

Sometimes
nothing, not philosophy
or religion,
art or knowledge,
is prudent,
provocative
or magnanimous enough
to provide illumination.
Sustenance.

Sometimes
bewilderment
is a lush, unsolvable labyrinth
leading deeper
into
ambiguity.

Speechless,
I apologized and left quickly,
and then,
after driving aimlessly for hours,
slept until dawn,
dreamless,
alongside the road,
in a field of wildflowers.

7
Born in 1920
in Czernowitz, Bukovina,
a German enclave in Romania,
Paul Antschel,
after
his parents were murdered in a German internment camp,
his father of starvation and disease,
his mother shot to death,
became Paul Ancel,
a grammar of sorrow
and intuitive echoes,
whose sole purpose was to illuminate, exfoliate,
and disavow
the precise meanings
of "Shot to death."

Became
a syntax of incendiary and irreverent machinations,
of anonymous conspiracies
seeking
a soupçon of consciousness,
the hovering angel's wing
of identity.

In other words,
a motherless/fatherless/countryless Jew,
who,
in Paris in 1944,
became Paul Celan,
a beleaguered,
fractured delirium,
adrift,
and in-between,
seeking
the same unsolvable answer
Camus sought
to the absurd paradox
of suicide.
Which is,
finally,
a judgment,
a gift
of consciousness.

8

There is much Osiris
has learned not to mind:
living with his girlfriend and baby daughter
in one room of her parents' house,
being unable to afford the van he drives us in,
the restaurants he takes us to.
After all,
serving is practical
and dignified.
One becomes
his habits, his confines.
"Here," he says,

"one marries neither politics nor God,
grows accustomed to families with many fathers,
here,
as Che Guevara said,
'even the illusion of progress is progress.'"

Perhaps
this is why
he and his father
wake in the middle of each night
and walk three miles to the sea
far from
the Militia Police and their psych wards
and electroshock treatments,
casting
wide and deep
into the cold rinse of dawn over Havana Harbor,
in order to know
the exquisite splash
and pull of the surprised line,
the shimmering silhouettes
of the essential.

Which
is why he believes
people will come
from as far as Santiago
to taste the gladness
of his strawberry ice cream.

9
Penelope and I,
observing

in the early morning ocean light
a fiery orange orb
at the far left side of the sky,
while
at the far right side,
no bigger than my thumb,
shy in profile,
the ghostly spider moon
dangling
by a spidery filament.
Suddenly
Penelope is barking
at an old man stumbling out of the beach entrance,
measuring
with a cane each small step.

Yes,
miles from town,
head tilted toward the waves,
as if listening for instruction,
the improbability
of an old man with a cane,
perhaps blind,
sensing
what we see,
a buck, doe and three yearlings
stepping out of the dunes,
all of us
suddenly
locked in a jittery vigilance,
turning one toward the other,
each,
incredible as it seems,

an industry of observation,
a tiny fragile pause,
ingenious scrap of discernment,
colliding
for a moment
before vanishing
back
into the bright, infinite
vagueness
from which we came.

Three

O one, o none, o no one, o you:
Where did the way lead when it led nowhere?
—PAUL CELAN

1

Sometimes
when something I fear
cannot tolerate
something I desire
I'll wince
and shudder
and shout out,
as if confronted
with an idea or thought or feeling
I cannot accept.
Then,
at the center of a pause
I never felt before,
a voice will remind me of things I do poorly,
mistakes I cannot forgive.

Sometimes
unable to breathe
or feel my hands or feet,
a void
inside me
slowly fills
with
the sobriety
and brilliance
of shame.

This is when
a black bird perches on my shoulder,
asking me to stop thinking
stop talking
and dreaming,
to stop,
simply
just
stop.

2

The big houses
on the dunes
certainly are provocative,
inorganic growths
endorsing peculiar and curious emblems and motifs.
Some see them
as museums of the exaggerated self,
impenetrable mausoleums,
though they provide employment,
taxes that pay
for our schools, hospitals and police.
Their enormous hedges and fences,
expansive gardens and lawns
are cared for by armies
of workers from Mexico,
Ecuador, Guatemala
and here,
whose music
the wind carries
over the waves.

Occasionally,
a figure appears

on a balcony or front lawn,
a face behind a lace curtain,
searching
the horizon
as if for a sign . . .

It's best not to wave,
we are strangers after all,
ciphers
equally temporal
and mystified,
which is why
Penelope and I so quickly pass by.

3
One Sunday morning
a used blue Ford station wagon
was parked under the big oak
instead of the gold Pontiac.
Knowing
it was not something
any of us
wanted to imagine ourselves inside,
Dad just shrugged.

Blue,
after all,
wasn't conceived billions of years ago out of asteroids,
isn't a symbol of balance and divine principles,
value measured in rarity,
malleable and ductile,
what Abraham was rich in,
Moses covered the Mercy Seat of the Ark of the Covenant with,
what triumph sealed itself in.

Blue
was the color of Mother's eyes
as she tried to smile
and then looked away
and sighed.

4
Flames, R said,
scraping the street and the sky
like black clouds
rising
everywhere around him
and his bereft foster mother
as they stood on the roof of her tenement,
watching Detroit burn,
July 1967.
He'd just graduated college,
was already ancient
and clandestine,
with everything and nothing beckoning,
and now *this*
flames
sweeping upward
out of windows and fire escapes,
out of stores and cars along 12th and Claremont,
like prayers, he said,
like pleas to a deaf and dumb God.

Twenty-two,
he was going to grad school in the fall
to study poetry — imagine that,
a bastard orphan Hart Crane
wanting to be so fine,

bearing witness to his own incineration,
his own sacrifice
amid the fires of hell...

all the while
his mother's voice
rising
on antediluvian wings,
singing,

this is all you need to know
to survive in this world
give up give up everything
enough times to reach God

5
The woman
from whom I ordered Dad's stone
insisted *Rest In Peace*
was more fitting than *In Last Relief.*

Yes,
but neither mother nor I
believed
that either
really fit.

There
amid pungent May lilacs,
cacophonous birds,
Dad's brother and two sisters, a few friends,
gathered
around a hole in the ground,

dark
and deep
as eternity.
No angels that I could see,
trumpets or weeping,
just a stuttering rabbi repeating things
God said
when no one was listening.
No hymns, psalms or locusts,
just tired sunlight,
the slightest rain.

6
Did he,
Hemingway,
believe
that
after all the grand schemes
and spectacles of hubris,
the gluttony
and wounds that wouldn't heal,
that after
all
that voracious appetite
and spiteful infidelity and sorrow
maybe
the moment
he placed the shotgun in his mouth
the dead would become virtuous and clean,
his father would stop visiting his dreams,
pleading for forgiveness . . .

Yes

maybe
finally
the pain would end,
silence would erase the ignominy,
the blame
and rage,
maybe
finally
he'd be able
to sleep.

7

Bokovina, Romania,
where Martin Buber imagined his Hasidic tales
and Celan and his mother were born,
is a region of outcomes
and aftermaths
without resolution,
a destination no longer on maps,
fallen, as he said,
into "historylessness,"
a place where
the graves of Jews speak to each other
in a lost language.

Occasionally,
with drugs and shock therapy,
Celan sought the truth "inside the madness,"
the almond of grief,
the beautiful seed
found inside his negative theology,
the living spasm and glimmer
that plead

not to be betrayed
or forgotten.

8
Death
is the most beautiful bullet
"in this pistol that always accompanies me"
Che Guevara said.
R wore Che's sullen, possessed, asthmatic face
on a T-shirt,
a face poisoned with self-loathing and pride,
a longing
to be sacrificed.

A face not unlike R's own,
staring straight through this world
into the next,
daring us
not to remember him.

9
The turtle crossing Old Stone Highway
this morning
may not yet
have arrived at its destination,
should one exist.
Perhaps
one shouldn't interfere
with the struggles of a species not his own?
Sisyphus's dilemma was human,
after all.
Sympathy
as ancient

and often hopeless
an enterprise
as instinct and desire.

Out here
in spring
a high frequency of wings,
the dissonance of unbridled wind,
the endless walking
and running along winding roads
and blind curves,
the wild uninhibited willfulness
of anxious new life.

Yesterday
a man riding his bike
was killed when a deer hit by a pickup
flew into him
from across the road.
Bad luck, Murphy's Law,
or a logic
so perverse
as to be absurd?

Perhaps
they shared,
this man and deer:
a love of fields of tall grass,
cul-de-sacs and back roads leading nowhere,
a belief in family,
loyalty
and the common good,
loved the dusk equally.

Four

> I can swim in existence, but for this mystical soaring
> I am too heavy.
> —SØREN KIERKEGAARD

1

The first
and only life I ever managed to save
was my own.
Twenty and indigent,
living in an attic
and caring for an invalid child,
I, following Nietzsche's strict code of ethics,
embraced the things
he believed worth living for:
"virtue, art, music, the dance, reason
and the mind . . ."
mad, delicate or divine things
that transfigure pain.
Yet
when the girl I loved wrote
saying she'd found someone else,
everything seemed unworthy.
I swallowed half a bottle of tranquilizers
and slit my left wrist,
then watched with cruel fascination
as my future
slowly abandoned me.

But fearing
the child's parents thinking me negligent,
and what the god I professed

not to believe in
would think of me,
I called for help.

2

My sons came to this tiny cemetery
under the windmill
to play tag
after music school across the street.
I come to walk among
the nearly illegible stones
of Puritan settlement-makers
and true-believers,
the Millers, Osbornes and Hedges,
our original neighbors.
To visit Mary Huntting,
dead June 5th 1779,
married over two hundred years to Nathan,
third cousin to Adeline S,
wife to Jeremiah T. Parsons Jr.
and the good Rev. Milford Osborne,
who no doubt provides guidance still.
Perhaps
it's best not to wonder
if their joy equaled their suffering,
what sins, if any, were forgiven,
if
they believed their arduous, brief lives
forged out of water, woods and stubborn skies
were worthy of gratitude.

Here,
under

these four fixed blades
stirring nothing but time,
within earshot of Main Street
and the summer uproar,
this quaint, beautiful place
offers no place to sit,
though my shadow
provides a little shade.

3
After
Dad died
everything flattened,
became meanwhile
and miscellaneous.
Mom went back to the same filing job
she worked as a girl,
while I got work on a roofing gang,
dumping truckloads of debris at a landfill
with a one-eyed black man named Willy,
who sang: "Even a cracked sink is a glory!
A castaway bed a sweetness!"
Nevertheless,
it was spring,
the birds, trees and lilacs exuberant,
the gardens prosperous
and grateful.
Hungry for praise,
eager to join
the ceremony of appetite
and delight,
I said goodbye
to all the things

that no longer belonged to me,
the tiny street and tinier house,
each wayward
and obliging fantasy
I once disappeared inside,
now waiting
impatiently
to belong to someone else.

4
Could R
in his last moments,
parked on a cliff overlooking the Pacific,
appreciate the strength of the will
that had taken him that far?
Could he see himself
as someone who'd known joy,
the wizardry
and reconstituted bliss
that lived in him
deeper
than the pain?

Did he recall with pleasure
the seventeen-year-old wunderkind
who played pieces
from Rachmaninoff's Piano Concerto no. 3
in a scholarship competition
in Tiger Stadium,
his among two hundred and fifty fingers
reawakening Beethoven,
the Beatles, Chopin and Liszt
as roaming judges

listened to his intricately shifting overtones
and hard cacophonous breath,
amid
the furious clapping . . .

Yes,
I'd like to think that
at the very end
he understood
he was more than
a blunt machine of misery.

5
Camus asks us to imagine Sisyphus happy,
in fact,
he says we must,
all is despair otherwise.
Well,
inside Dad's tough-guy squint
lived the tiniest hint of glee.
Indeed,
even when he puckered his fat pugnacious lower lip,
stood feet wide apart,
as if expecting a blow,
a judgment from God,
I could find
deep
in his black shtetl don't-mess-with-me eyes
the place where I lived,
if not valued
at least not judged.
Yes,
when I wince
I see myself only in my eyes.

Once,
on New Year's Eve,
in the lobby of the Waldorf Astoria Hotel,
Dad stood tossing nickels to bellhops,
a jubilant pint-sized baggy-panted Rockefeller,
swaggering
amidst the marble and potted ferns,
the colorful ladies and well-bred men,
not the man who died bankrupt
and penniless,
but a self-anointed king.

And then,
later, in Times Square,
he lifted me aloft in his arms,
pointing at the ball
dropping
out of one golden speculation
into the next,
the two of us,
father and son
counting the seconds left in 1953
. . . *eight . . . seven . . . six . . .*
among thousands
singing
Happy New Year
and *God Bless America.*

6
Once,
in 1986, in late spring,
one of Hemingway's granddaughters
called to ask
if I was the poet who'd written

about her grandfather's house in Key West.
I said yes
and she asked
if my father had also killed himself,
the poem seemed to say so.
Her voice,
sunken and forlorn,
sounded weary
of speaking intimately
to strangers.
Yes, I said,
essentially,
he was tired
of suffering the illusion of success,
the sorrow
of impotence.
Well, she asked, was I
also obsessed
with the idea of suicide?
I tried hard not to be, I said,
and we both laughed.
She was a painter, she said,
and a few other things,
but mostly a Hemingway.
Did I know what I wanted
from her grandfather?
Once, I said, I believed
it was rhapsody,
the art of self-invention,
turning anger
and despair into music,
speaking simply
and truthfully.
Now, I said,

I understood
it was something
more private
and essential:
permission to live.

7
The metaphysics
of suffering
prefers paralysis,
the vanity of shame,
not inquiry,
certainly
not Celan's negative theology
that owned
no underlying schemes.
Celan,
also a revolutionary
of sundered words,
a true believer
of overthrowing
the governing principles
of the forlorn.

Yes,
deep
inside the wound
of his mother's and father's souls,
a prophecy
he couldn't escape,
anchored
by
the dark anvil of death.

At night
in bed
I see him climbing onto the bridge,
looking down at the flowing Seine,
and then,
one last time,
up at the fires of his cold city,
pausing
to appreciate the "radiance"
of his petrified blessing,
the patience of the persecuted past,
he, a faithful husband and father,
here,
for a moment longer,
among the curious,
the frivolous
and the savage,

and then
the falling
and the tiniest splash.

8
Osiris
is driving us up the side of a mountain
to an orchid farm in Soroa,
saying, "This is the most magical place
in this disappointed land."
Indeed,
a glittering garden of 20,000 orchid plants
winding up and around
respectful roots
and ornamental ferns and trees,

stubbornly alive butterflies,
80 species of birds
and the world's smallest frog.
A sweetness
overflowing
the beautiful names
our guide, Hermosa, sings:
Paphiopedilum, Acacallis cyanea,
Vanda Blue, Brassia-Peggy-Ruth,
Phalaenopsis-Mystik,
and Waterfall Pansy . . .
and there,
inside this labyrinth of hot light,
these phosphorous spheres,
us,
a man and wife and two fervent young men,
a family like any other,
relishing
the capacity
of such improbable blossoms,
each
a promise of splendor,
another hour of fever,
a voluptuous awakening,
a refuge
from the despair
stowed in the mind.

9
Now,
from across the house,
the booming voice of my sixteen-year-old son
announces his belief

in the law and right of succession,
the beginning of his reign.
Already too big for this house,
it conspires with a future
that is his alone.
My wife,
a sculptor,
looks up from her porcelain cakes
arrayed over the living room table,
which, even
with the dead birds and beetles
and tiny people writhing on top,
are festive enough.
While I,
standing in the kitchen,
pondering questions about guilt,
satisfaction and lunch,
remember leaning against
the sycamore in our front yard
twenty-six years ago,
trying to imagine a family
inside the house I just bought,
a future prolific enough
to contain squawking blackbirds,
flying deer
and a notion
as mysterious and improbable,
as fragrant
and luxurious
as happiness.

ACKNOWLEDGMENTS

Some of these poems have previously appeared in different form and with different titles in the following magazines, to whose editors grateful acknowledgment is made:

Epiphany, *Five Points*, the *Gettysburg Review*, the *Harvard Review*, the *Kenyon Review*, *The New Yorker*, the *Paris Review*, *Ploughshares*, *Poetry*, Poets.org Poem-a-Day, *Provincetown Arts*, *Slate*, and the *Southern Review*.

I wish to thank friends who read these poems in various stages:
Carl Dennis, James Lasdun, Robert Pinsky,
Grace Schulman, Ronald Sharp, Drenka Willen,
and especially my editor Jill Bialosky.